in grey

volume ii of a silent trilogy

by

starling

No part of this publication may be reproduced, stored in a retrieval system, or transmitted in any form or by any means—electronic, mechanical, photocopying, recording, or otherwise—without the prior written permission of the publisher.

Published by Untold Imprint
www.sdarling-art.com

ISBN: 978-1-7641672-1-5
Printed in: Australia

THIS IS A WORK OF POETRY AND PHILOSOPHY. ANY RESEMBLANCE TO REAL PERSONS, LIVING OR DEAD, IS PURELY COINCIDENTAL.

*a minute of silence drowned in the
restless echoes of a world on the edge*

this is a collection of moments
etched in the unseen voids between the in-between—
some through premeditated thoughts,
others through confusion,
and in the quiet hum
of a world that no longer makes sense.
not in order,
not in narrative,
but as fragments
shaped by silence,
discomfort,
and reflection.

in grey is the second of three.
this is not a story.
it is a pause in the middle of thought.
you are not asked to follow it.
only to feel its edges,
and listen to what it leaves unsaid.

this is not just a book.
it is a thought in between,
meant to be experienced,
not explained.

i. ghost

some nights i feel so close to figuring it out,
as if the answers are just beyond my grasp,
hovering on the edge of my consciousness,
teasing me with their elusive presence.

in the quiet of the night, when the world sleeps,
i wrestle with the mysteries of existence,
pondering the meaning of life and the universe,
and searching for truth amidst the shadows.

but just when i think i have found the key,
the puzzle shifts and the pieces scatter,
leaving me staring at a new arrangement,
one that makes less sense than before.

i am forced to begin again,
retracing steps i thought i'd already taken,
knowing the path will change beneath my feet,
and the answers will keep moving further away.

yet still, i follow —
drawn by the promise of that almost-moment,
that fleeting point where everything aligns,
before it all unravels, and i am back at the start.

i have a deeply hidden and inarticulate desire
for something beyond this world, a longing
that stirs within me like a restless sea,
and whispers of realms unseen and unexplored.

in the quiet corners of my soul, it lingers,
a silent yearning that defies explanation,
a longing for transcendence and transformation,
and a yearning to touch the divine.

for in the depths of my being, i sense
that there is more to life than meets the eye,
that beyond the confines of this earthly realm
there lies a reality beyond comprehension.

and so i find myself drawn to the unknown,
to the mysteries that lie beyond the veil,
seeking solace in the embrace of the infinite,
and yearning to uncover the secrets of existence.

but even as i reach for the stars,
i am reminded of the limitations of my understanding,
and the futility of trying to grasp the ineffable,
for some truths are meant to remain shrouded in mystery.

and yet, in my longing, there is a kind of beauty —
a recognition of the vastness of the universe,
and the infinite possibilities that lie within it,
a reminder that even in the darkest of nights,
there is always a glimmer of hope.

why is the unknown so familiar,
a paradox that haunts the corridors of thought,
as if we have wandered these uncharted paths before
and yet cannot recall the journey?

in the depths of our consciousness lies
a reservoir of ancient wisdom,
a repository of knowledge and experience
that slips beyond the reach of time and space.

when we confront the unknown
there is a strange recognition,
a feeling that we have been here before,
and that the answers hover just beyond our grasp.

perhaps the familiarity of the unknown
is not a ghost of past lives or forgotten memories,
but the quiet proof of something shared —
the universality of being human.

we are all explorers
in the unending expedition of life,
drifting through uncharted waters,
meeting the same mysteries in different disguises.

and so, when we stand before the unknown,
we are not strangers in a strange land,
but fellow travellers in the same vast dark,
bound by the search for something
we may never name.

silent madness —
a contradiction that breathes,
a storm hidden beneath glassy waters,
its waves felt only in the marrow.

it moves through the mind
like smoke in a locked room,
curling into thoughts,
blurring the line between knowing and unravelling.

perhaps it is the weight of questions
that refuse to be named,
or the pulse of some ancient dread
that hums beneath all human hearts.

perhaps it is the shadow of mortality
pressed against the veil of our days,
the faint outline of whatever waits
beyond the horizon we cannot cross.

silent madness is both mirror and void —
reminding us how fragile the mind is,
how reality is only a thin thread
stretched over an abyss we pretend not to see.

and yet, in its darkness,
there is an austere beauty,
as if the chaos within us
is also a map to something vast.

for it is in tracing these fault lines inward
that we sometimes step through
and find ourselves
somewhere we have always been.

because at the time i looked at her, she began to fade —
not with the grace of twilight,
but like smoke dispersing into air,
a vanishing act written into the fabric of being.

what is beauty but a shadow on the wall,
bright for a breath, then gone,
leaving only the ache of absence
where presence once resided?

yet her outline clings to the recess of my mind,
not whole, not steady,
but fractured, trembling,
as if memory itself were conspiring to erase her.

in this fading i see no comfort,
only the cruel reminder
that nothing we touch is ours to keep —
not faces, not moments,
not even the echoes of our own desire.

still, i look back into that silence,
and the hollow where she once stood
burns brighter than her presence ever did —
proof that what vanishes
often marks us more deeply
than what remains.

the feeling of living in between,
a spectral realm where shadows blur and bleed,
where certainty dissolves into the mist
and choices fracture into ghostly mirrors.

for what is life but a trembling balance,
a tightrope stretched across an unseen void?
we drift in twilight, half-formed,
never entirely present, never entirely gone.

time here is thin as paper,
each moment folding into the next,
echoes chasing echoes down a corridor
with no first sound, no final silence.

and in this in-between a truth emerges —
not comfort, but a darker clarity:
that meaning is only the shadow cast
by doubt against an endless wall.

so linger here, suspended and unsure,
a figure carved from half-light,
neither ascending nor falling,
but endlessly becoming unfinished.

some nights i fall in reverse, a quiet plunge
into the depths where time unravels,
where shadows bend against themselves
and the edges of reality come undone.

for what is falling but the memory
of every step we thought was forward —
a spiral carved in silence,
repeating what was never escaped.

in this backward drift, i touch the bones
of fears i buried long ago,
only to find them restless,
gnawing still beneath the soil of thought.

and if there is a light, it does not save —
it flickers like a false star,
a brief glimmer in the void,
reminding me the fall has no end.

find me at midnight, alone inside my mind,
where shadows lengthen into endless corridors,
and thought itself becomes a labyrinth
with no map, no exit, only echoes.

for what is midnight but the unmasking hour,
when silence sharpens, and the hidden things
crawl from the marrow of the soul,
demanding to be named in the dark.

i wrestle not to win, but to endure,
to let the fractures show their jagged light,
to see if the pieces, scattered and strange,
form something i have yet to recognize.

and in this solitude, perhaps a truth —
that wholeness was never the aim at all,
only the haunting knowledge of myself,
a shadow walking beside the shadow i am.

it's the universe, and still you blame the stars,
pinning your sorrow to constellations,
as if their cold geometry could explain
the fractures that bloom within your chest.

but what are stars if not indifferent fires,
burning in silence across an endless void,
witnesses who neither condemn nor forgive,
who turn away even as you plead for meaning?

yet still you search their frozen faces,
seeking fate in their scattered design,
a pattern to absolve your trembling hands
from the choices carved in shadow.

blame not the stars —
they have no language for your grief.
instead, descend into the quiet within,
where truth flickers like a fragile flame,
unsteady, yet yours to bear alone.

the past is more than what we leave behind,
it lingers in the marrow, in the silence
between two breaths, in the shadows
that stretch longer than the body casting them.

it seeps into the present like forgotten rain,
staining the soil with memories half-buried,
and even as we walk away,
our footsteps echo back from corridors unseen.

perhaps the past is not behind us at all,
but beneath us, above us, within —
a labyrinth that folds and unfolds,
carving paths we mistake for choice.

the past is more than what we leave behind;
it is what follows, what watches,
what waits in the corner of every dream,
reminding us that nothing ever truly goes.

and then they were just strangers with all each other's secrets,
a silence heavier than words could bear,
a distance carved not by time alone
but by the weight of knowing too much.

what is intimacy, if not a dangerous pact —
to hand someone the keys to the locked rooms
of your soul, only to watch them vanish,
leaving the doors ajar, shadows spilling out?

in the end, they carried each other like ghosts,
not in presence, but in the burden of memory,
the quiet ache of being both known and forsaken,
a mirror cracked but still reflecting.

and then they were just strangers with all each other's
secrets —

a haunting truth: nothing binds us closer
than the things we cannot take back,
and nothing divides us deeper than being seen.

i'm made of all the days you never saw,
not just the ones you claim as memory —
the hours that bled quietly into the dark,
the heartbeats no one cared enough to count.

what you see is only the surface flicker,
a shadow cast by something vaster, hidden,
threads woven through the fabric of a time
too immense for any gaze to hold.

in those forgotten moments lies the weight
that shapes me more than presence ever could —
not the days displayed like trophies to the world,
but the silent intervals where nothing spoke.

so do not measure me by what survives the light;
the truth is stitched into the hours erased,
and if you would seek me, seek me there —
in the quiet that devours, yet sustains.

ii. gather

i'm full of stories i won't ever speak of,
a library of untold tales hidden within —
each one a chapter of my inner world,
a secret kept safe from prying eyes.

in the depths of my soul, these stories dwell,
unseen and unheard, yet potent and alive —
each one a thread in the tapestry of my being,
weaving together the fabric of my existence.

but why do i keep these stories locked away?
what compels me to guard them with such insistence?
perhaps it is fear — fear of judgment or rejection,
or perhaps it is simply the nature of the human condition.

for we are all, in some ways,
prisoners of our own stories —
bound by the narratives we create for ourselves,
and the roles we play in the theatre of life,
afraid to deviate from the script we have written.

but in the silence of these untold stories,
there is also freedom — freedom to imagine,
to dream, to create without constraint,
to explore the boundless possibilities of existence.

so let us honour these stories, these hidden treasures,
and cherish the richness they bring to our lives —
for in their mystery lies the essence of our humanity,
and the potential for endless discovery.

there are rooms inside me
i only enter in silence.
they have no doors,
only echoes —
and somewhere in the distance,
my truest self
is still waiting
with open arms.

everything i could never tell you
drifts in orbit around my skull,
a constellation of moments
that could never survive the pull of this world.

they burn in silence,
their light reaching you long after it left me,
trapped in the slow gravity
between what was felt and what could be spoken.

some are shards of collapsed stars,
cold and precise,
cutting the palms of my thoughts
each time i reach for them.

others are black holes,
pulling the breath from my chest
whenever your name
touches the edges of my mind.

if i loosed them into the air between us,
space itself would recoil,
and the ground beneath us
would not hold steady.

so i let them circle,
unseen,
until they fade into a darkness
only i will ever know —
and you will only ever feel
in the tremor of my silence.

hold back the world from me,
or perhaps hold me from the world —
i can no longer tell
which one isn't ready.

its noise seeps into my thoughts,
its colours run beyond their borders,
and i can't decide
if i'm seeing too much
or not nearly enough.

i drift between refuge and exile,
the quiet corners of my mind
a sanctuary and a prison
in the same breath.

each step toward the threshold
feels like walking
in two directions at once.
maybe the world waits for me,
or maybe it doesn't notice at all.

maybe readiness is an illusion —
a story we tell ourselves
to delay the inevitable crossing.
in the end,
it doesn't matter
who is waiting for whom.

the meeting will come
when it comes,
and both of us
will be unprepared.

i feel as if i was made to understand,
but not to be understood —
a strange design, as if the architect of my being
left out the language others might read.

i drift through the sea of humanity
like a deep-sea creature glimpsed only in shadows,
aware of the currents, the pull of unseen tides,
yet dwelling where light cannot follow.

in the chambers of my mind, i hold
maps of places no one else has walked,
truths stitched together from fragments
the world has not yet learned to name.

and though i reach for connection,
my words dissolve before they arrive —
whispers spoken underwater,
warped beyond recognition.

in this solitude, there is a strange power —
to move unseen through the labyrinth,
to carry the forbidden knowledge of my own making,
to exist beyond the reach of their comprehension.

perhaps i am not meant to be known at all,
but only to haunt the edges of understanding,
where reality thins,
and the shape of me cannot fully take form.

i don't want to forget, i want to be okay remembering,
to let each thought linger not as burden but as testament,
where moments, good and ill, are stitched
into the fragile seams of my psyche.

in the recesses of mind, shadows outweigh the light,
laughter arrives only as echo,
entangled with whispers of regret,
until i can no longer tell them apart.

to remember — is it not the most human paradox?
to stitch meaning into fractures,
knowing the fabric will always tear again,
yet calling the ruin by the name of truth.

memory, a canvas frayed and colourless,
stretched thin across a crooked frame.
it does not preserve, it corrodes —
and in the corrosion we mistake permanence.

what strength is needed to face not forgetting,
but clarity —
clarity that steals comfort,
that exposes faces, words, and rooms
which belong only to absence now.

so i remain, drifting upon recollection,
a tide that carries both solace and suffocation.
and i wonder —
if remembering is how we endure,
or how we disappear more completely.

i get homesick for places that don't exist,
for worlds washed in the shadows of dreams,
where reality blurs and fantasy reigns,
and the boundaries of thought dissolve.

in the quiet depths of my soul, i wander,
seeking solace in the embrace of the unreal,
finding refuge in the sanctuary of what never was,
as if my heart yearns for something beyond the tangible.

what draws me to these imagined realms,
these landscapes built from absence and desire?
perhaps it is the promise of freedom —
to live unbound by what is real.

or perhaps it is the ache of knowing
that the truest places are the ones
we can never stand within.

so i return to them in sleep,
to the corners of unreality that feel like home,
homesick for the worlds i cannot prove,
but which somehow feel more real than this.

inside my head, a picture unravels,
a vast geometry of thought
that refuses stillness.
it twists across the dark
like rivers breaking their banks,
overflowing any shape
i try to give them.

i have tried to contain them —
to press them into lines,
to bind them in order —
yet they return, heavier,
as if thought itself conspires
to undo its own silence.

inward, it is a hall of mirrors,
each reflection bending the next,
until i can no longer name
which shadow began the turning.
clarity arrives only to collapse,
like glass struck once
and left to spider endlessly.

and i wonder —
if the mind is a sanctuary or a snare,
if the endless circling is a search
or only its own punishment.
so let the picture remain unfinished,
a ghost etched on the walls within —
for it is not what i grasp that defines me,
but what slips away,
haunting the edges of thought,
refusing to be stilled.

as i fill the blank pages of this book,
i am reminded of the passage of time,
and the endless possibilities that stretch ahead
in this quiet act of expression and discovery.

each word becomes a brushstroke
on the fragile canvas of existence,
each sentence a faint melody
threading itself through the silence between thoughts.

i weave together fragments of experience,
a tapestry stitched with both meaning and absence.
yet as i write, i am met by the limits of language —
how can ink translate the weight of a moment,
the slow collapse of feeling into thought,
when the essence of it slips
through the cracks of every phrase?

and still, in the act of writing,
there is solace —
for creation is both wound and remedy,
a mirror that shows me to myself,
and binds me closer to what I cannot name.

so let me continue to fill these pages,
knowing they will never hold the whole.
perhaps the meaning lies not in capturing everything,
but in the attempt itself —
in the quiet trace left behind
when silence claims the rest.

i look at the blank paper with endless possibilities,
and crave to destroy the beauty of its simplicity—
to spill untold stories across its innocent surface,
to scar its purity with the ink of my unrest.

a pang in my chest, a quiet hunger,
to mar the whiteness with the weight of experience,
to let silence collapse into language,
to answer the void that demands to be filled.

and so i relent,
defiling the stillness with the noise of being,
unleashing a torrent of thought and shadow,
watching them writhe into crooked patterns on the page.

yet even in surrender, hesitation lingers—
a fear of staining beauty with imperfection,
of never again reclaiming the stillness
that lived before the first word.

but in the act of creation,
there is catharsis—
a rupture that rends the silence open,
transforming the void into something alive.

so let the ink bleed, let the page bruise,
for in the destruction of simplicity
there emerges a strange and jagged beauty—
a trembling proof that what is broken
is often more human than what is whole.

why would she make calls out the blue,
disturbing the calm lake of mind's repose,
sending ripples through the still surface
until reflection itself begins to break?

is it loneliness guiding her hand,
or thoughts that flare like sudden stars,
compelling her to bridge the void
with the fragile thread of voice?

perhaps she seeks to gather the frayed
edges of a bond once taut, now loosened,
or wake the buried fragments of memory—
dragons sleeping under dusted gold.

we wonder, because we cannot help
searching in others the echoes of ourselves—
our fears, our hungers, our quiet whims.
but sometimes there is no reason at all:

she calls not from need, nor from intent,
but to remind us, with one sudden ring,
that silence is never entirely ours.

for all the people who think i'm writing
about them, i am—though not of love,
nor of pain, nor those brief illusions
we mistake for meaning.
it isn't about joy or grief,
or the truths we chase until they turn to smoke.
it is about what remains, and all between—
the grey expanse that stretches without end.

in these murky depths of being,
we stumble through contradictions,
half-formed truths spun from fractured hours,
from dreams that never fully wake.
we wander a labyrinth folding inward,
where meaning devours itself in shadow,
and every answer arrives wearing a mask.

so if you find yourself within these lines,
know it is not you i've written,
but the space that hums between us—
that thin divide where light falters,
and darkness leans in close.
for every reflection is both you
and not you at once.

is it my fault that you're lost, wandering
through corridors you built yourself—
walls sewn from longing,
doors sealed with the weight of unspoken need?

you chase the light, but shadows bend it,
fracturing truth into mirages of hope.
and what is fault, if not the hollow word
we reach for when reason fails to hold?

paths diverge without intention,
threads snarl by hands unseen.
in your silence, i hear the question unasked—
a soundless plea that no answer could calm.

perhaps we are all lost, each in our turn,
drawn toward horizons that vanish as we near.
so do not ask who bears the blame—
in this brief and trembling span of life,
we are only wanderers tracing shadows,
searching constellations that fade with the dawn.

the road you've led me down is too long,
a path unraveling into shadowed depths,
each step heavier than the last,
each mile a silence i cannot name.

for what is distance but the echo
of burdens we pretend to bear with grace,
while hope flickers faintly—
a star that may already be dead.

in the half-light of this endless trek,
i question the turns, the unseen hands
that shaped this journey into a labyrinth,
a horizon always retreating, never reached.

perhaps this is the truth of roads—
not endings, but continuations,
circles winding back upon themselves,
teaching nothing, and teaching everything.

so i walk on, though the path dissolves,
unsure if i am moving forward,
or only deeper into the dark,
where meaning itself begins to blur.

i want to go up there, beyond the reach
of earth's slow chains and brittle bones,
into a realm where shadows dissolve
into deeper shadow—where stars are not guides
but wounds torn open in the sky.

for what is life but the ache to ascend,
to climb the invisible ladder of silence,
to touch the cold pulse of the cosmos
and vanish into the question it hums.

yet even as the night invites escape,
a whisper claws at me—
that in seeking the infinite above,
i betray the ground that bears my weight.

still, i rise—if only in thought—
drawn toward the quiet where meaning falters,
toward the edge where becoming and ending
blur into the same unspoken truth.

everyone is blinded when the view is amazing,
drowned in brilliance that erases sight,
a radiance so sharp it carves away
the contours of what lies beneath.

for what is splendor but a mask of fire,
a brightness that silences the shadows,
hiding their patient shapes
just beyond the edge of knowing.

in the flood of light, we mistake clarity
for blindness—wonder for truth—
our vision consumed by shimmer,
our awe turned quietly against us.

yet perhaps blindness has its own design,
a mercy threaded through the dazzle—
a warning that beauty deceives,
that behind every shining horizon
waits the unseen, unnamed, and real.

we weren't the closest when i wrote this,
a faint inscription carved across the silence,
each line a measure of the widening gulf
that stretched between two shadows once aligned.

for what is closeness but a fragile thread,
pulled thin beneath the weight of passing time,
snapping softly where no ear could hear,
leaving only echoes where voices used to meet.

in the hollow spaces of unsaid words,
the truth emerges—cold, unadorned:
connection was always more fragile
than either of us dared to name.

yet distance, too, becomes a mirror,
revealing what nearness sought to hide—
that even in absence, something lingers,
uncertain, unfinished, quietly alive.

iii. gloom

disturbingly relaxing,
where all sense dissolves—
what remains is the quiet
of one's own void.

on the edge of the earth,
memory loosens its hold;
what once was adored
now drifts, unnamed,
into the calm
that forgets itself.

another cold, emotionless morning alone.
of all the memories that remain,
this is the one i wish to release.
yet even as it dissolves,
it lingers—
a silent presence in the corner,
unwilling to leave.

in this comforting room of black
i shape a way of seeing—
a vision born from absence,
where silence becomes instruction.
i learned more here
than some dare
to discover.

in the lifeless night,
oh... these dreams—
full moon glooms
searching for truth.
i lie awake,
and it intensifies
something unnamed.
i liked how it felt—
the ache before meaning.

as no words
were spoken,
we simply remained—
still, suspended.
it began to fade
before we knew,
our voices drifting away
with the morning snow.

when i undressed her, i began with her words.
her soul unfolded—intricate, fractured,
more complex than anything i'd known.
she said she was damaged,
scarred by the past, afraid of the future.
but it didn't make me leave.
i stayed long enough
to learn the shape of her ruin.
it was never about saving her—
only to see
how far the cracks would reach
before she realised
my hands were breaking too.

i fantasize about refusing the apologies
that will never come—
in dim corridors where memory bends,
and justice belongs to me alone.

in this imagined tribunal,
i am both judge and sentence,
weighing their trespass
against the silence they left behind.

there are no second chances here,
no comfort in contrition—
only the cold satisfaction
of a door closed and bolted from within.

apologies are ghosts,
and ghosts do not speak.
the past decays where it fell,
and i will not unearth it.

rejection becomes the verdict,
unyielding, precise—
not forgiveness, not forgetting,
but the quiet reclamation
of what was once mine.

all she sought, was never enough.
in the depths of her longing, she wandered,
through corridors of desire that stretched endlessly,
where each doorway promised but never delivered.

she chased after dreams like shadows in the night,
but they slipped through her hands like smoke,
leaving her clutching fragments of absence,
yearning for something she could never name.

she was a seeker of the strange and the beautiful,
a pilgrim lost in the vast interior of her soul.
yet no matter how far she travelled,
the horizon folded back into distance,
and the destination dissolved into mirage.

so she roamed the labyrinth of her own desires,
a nomad of the intangible,
finding solace in the peculiar and the absurd,
where strangeness gave her freedom,
and absurdity whispered its truth.

for all she sought was never enough,
but perhaps it was in the endless seeking—
not the finding—
that she finally met herself.

unexpectedly,
with the realm in mind,
somehow
caught between
space and time—

a pause that stretched
beyond intention,
where nothing moved,
yet everything changed.

trying to find
the things i'm feeling,
while heartbeats resonate
in the obscure.
i crave an overdose
on this love.

thought it was going up
while falling—
the way it was,
i wasn't used to.
i hope you find
a soft place to land.

blank spaces
fill my instants,
one's thoughts
drowning in realness.
beneath the surface,
i'll find my sanity,
folded within
a silence too aware
of its own echo.

i looked at her much less often than i wanted to—
a confession carved from restraint,
a hunger muted by the fear
of being seen too clearly.

desire burns in silence,
a quiet fire that lights the mind
yet consumes the self in shadows.
her presence lingered like smoke,
curling through corridors of thought,
a haunting that refused to fade.

to look was never enough,
for eyes are liars,
and what they touch they cannot keep.
perhaps to see her fully
would be to unravel the boundary
between longing and despair.

and so the question remains—
was it mercy to look away,
or cowardice to never truly see?
in the end, i cannot tell
whether my restraint preserved me,
or only deepened the absence i tried to escape.

in the caverns of memory,
i savour a bitter refrain,
remembering how love used to taste—
a haunting strain.

once nectar,
sweet on the tongue's eager feast,
now a bitter residue—
a love that slowly ceased.

the flavour lingers,
a spectral bitterness remains,
as shadows dance
through the corridors of old pains.

the taste of passion
now a bitter aftertaste,
in the remnants of a love
that couldn't withstand the haste.

on the palate of nostalgia,
the bitterness persists—
a ghostly reminder
of love's melancholic twists.

the sweetness faded,
leaving only a bitter trace.
i remember how love used to taste
in the darkened space.

in the labyrinth of existence,
i danced on the edge of twisted fate,
tracing the elusive contours of the end
before its arrival—

where the beauty of the unravelling journey
tangled with the darkness
lurking in the shadows.

if you try to understand, you can hear
how i fantasize about not being here,
in the quiet whispers of my soul's lament,
and the echoes of my silent screams.

for beneath the surface of my stoic facade,
lies a tumult of emotions, raw and unfiltered,
a kaleidoscope of dreams and desires,
that yearn for expression, for release.

in the depths of my longing, i find wisdom,
for it is in acknowledging our darkest truths,
that we find the light to guide us forward,
and the strength to face our deepest fears.

so listen closely, and you will hear
the wisdom of my words, spoken in hushed tones,
for in the vulnerability of my confession,
lies the courage to confront my own mortality.

and though the path ahead may be uncertain,
i take solace in the knowledge
that by embracing the fullness of my existence,
i can find peace in the midst of chaos.

in a darkened mind,
trying to find the thing i'm feeling,
i'll find a new place to be from.

illumination of unknown thoughts
plays a silent whisper
in the ear of the unaware.

look at her falling,
draped in the cold of moonlight,
the air thinning around her.
does she even know
what she's falling for?

she drifts through shadows
that have no ground,
chasing something
she's already lost.

perhaps she falls
not for love,
but for the absence of it—
a silence
that feels like home.

in the shadows cast by fear's relentless grip,
we stumble blindly through the mist—
a world besieged by chaos and despair,
where hope's faint ember strains to survive.

the echoes of our cries move through corridors
of uncertainty and dread.
silent spectres haunt our waking hours,
and nightmares follow long after we have fled.

each day arrives with burdens we cannot name,
while the weight of the past
clings like chains to our skin.
whispers of what is coming grow louder,
and the shadows deepen.

in every corner,
darkness waits—
a shape without form,
an unknown we cannot see.

we search for a guiding light
but remain bound to this place.
yet even here,
in the deepest night,
something resilient still survives—
a flicker in the heart of those who fight,
a small, persistent flame.

we long for each other, but only in absence—
when one vanishes, the hunger sharpens,
and the empty air becomes electric,
charged with what cannot be touched.

for what is desire but a ghost of presence,
a fragile spark kept alive by distance,
a flame that flares brightest
only in the hollow left behind.

in separation, the heart invents its music,
a melody born of echo and ache,
sweeter in the void than in the touch,
truer in the silence than in the sound.

and so we learn this paradox of love—
that it flickers not in the constant light,
but in the spaces where shadow gathers,
where the absence is more vivid than the flesh.

it'll be a long time before you see me again,
he said, and the words sank heavy into the night,
a vow cast beneath the false infinity
of stars that flicker like lies.

such words do not vanish—
they hang like autumn's last leaf,
trembling until the cruel wind
decides its ending.

what is absence, if not a shadow
that grows longer with each passing day,
filling the room where laughter once lived,
remaking memory into a ghost?

distance does not empty—
it reshapes, distorts,
turning vivid colours into pale sepia,
etching presence into hollow silhouettes.

and yet absence is never empty:
it is presence inverted,
a light you cannot see but feel,
like a sun eclipsed,
its fire still burning behind the darkened veil.

so let the distance stretch,
let time unravel into years unnamed;
for every parting drags behind it
a thread of return—
whether in flesh, or in memory,
or in dreams that refuse to die.

iv. glitch

i like to go places where i don't belong—
a confession spoken to the dark,
as if absence itself were listening.

belonging feels too much like a cage,
its bars forged from expectation,
its locks fastened by the hands of others.

yet in the places that reject me,
i find a strange kind of freedom—
a freedom born not of welcome,
but of dissonance,
where every step feels stolen
and every breath unsettles the air.

perhaps i wander not to discover,
but to dissolve—
to test the edges of myself
against landscapes that do not call my name,
to learn what lingers
when nothing around me offers recognition.

for what if belonging is not found,
but endlessly deferred,
a mirage that recedes
each time we draw near?

then let me keep walking into the wrong rooms,
haunting the thresholds of unfamiliar doors—
for in never belonging,
i come closest to myself.

a minute of quiet disturbance
in a loud and shouting world—
a paradoxical anomaly
that defies comprehension,
like a glitch in the matrix,
disrupting the status quo
and leaving us unsettled
in its wake.

in the chaos of our existence,
where noise reigns supreme,
this moment of silence
is an irregularity,
a disagreeing note
in the symphony of life,
a reminder of the fragility
of our reality.

and yet, in its strangeness,
there is a kind of beauty,
a surreal quality
that captivates the imagination—
as if we have stumbled
upon a hidden entry
to a realm beyond the confines
of our understanding.

in this brief interlude,
time seems to stretch and warp,
and the boundaries between worlds
blur and dissolve,
leaving us suspended
in a liminal space,
where anything is possible
and nothing is as it seems.

so let us embrace
this moment of quiet disturbance
and revel in its strangeness,
for in its passing nature
lies the potential
for otherworldliness and change.

a labyrinth of echoes in the night,
moving side by side with neon shadows
on a paving stone street.
silhouette palm trees
and strange symphonies—
the mystery of dawn is where we meet.

she converses in a sunlit daze,
strange demeanour as she dances,
a peculiar opportunity,
so i take my chance.

being quiet
doesn't mean i have nothing to say—
it means you're not ready
to hear my thoughts.

silence is not absence,
it is a blade
forged in the dark,
waiting for the right throat.

write something, then i might erase it.
i love it, then i hate it—like to recite
to always be yourself,
but the sentiment
makes me feel like
i'm someone different.

a lot of people know me,
but they don't know me well.
and in the quiet after,
i'm not sure
if i want them to.

i've been here before, but it's different—
nothing like i'm used to.
sometimes i don't know
how to feel; feeling nothing is also a feeling,
and it doesn't mean it's not real.

we're trapped in the blank verse we cannot write.
we speak in pauses,
letting the silence
finish our sentences,
as if the words themselves
were afraid to exist.

i'm hiding where you can see me—
a paradox wrapped in glass,
my outline clear, my substance blurred,
the truth flickering behind the surface.

i haunt the edges of the ordinary,
a shadow stitched to daylight,
wearing the skin of the familiar
while my bones hum with elsewhere.

hiding is not absence,
but a strange kind of seeking—
a search for shelter beneath exposure,
a desire to vanish and be found in the same breath.

i do not hide from fear,
but from the crude light that strips things bare;
i hide in the folds of silence,
where recognition is more than being looked at.

perhaps it is not weakness but craft—
a quiet defiance against a world
that mistakes seeing for knowing.

and so i remain here,
in plain sight yet out of reach,
a still figure in an open room,
waiting for the one who sees through glass.

the things that i need are not what is needed—
a riddle spoken in the hollow night,
its voice a whisper blurred by shadowed walls,
a meaning folding back upon itself.

what lies beneath such fractured syllables?
a warning, or a hunger without name?
a lament dressed as prophecy, perhaps,
or only the echo of my own unrest.

for what we reach for often fades to smoke,
desire casting shapes we call necessity—
yet touch them, and they vanish into mist,
leaving only the weight of empty hands.

perhaps no answer waits beneath the phrase;
perhaps the puzzle is the truth itself:
that need and want are mirrors, each reflecting
a void that grows the closer we approach.

maybe it's the hunger itself that keeps us alive.

feeling this in a slightly different way,
like walking through a room i know by heart
yet finding every object faintly altered,
the chairs turned inward, the windows breathing.

voices drift like mist, half-formed,
their syllables dissolving before meaning takes shape,
and time itself seems to hesitate—
a pendulum caught mid-swing,
neither here nor there, but trembling.

dreams seep into the walls,
their shadows curling at the edges of my sight,
and i wonder if i've woken at all
or simply stepped deeper into another layer.

and again i return—
feeling this in a slightly different way,
as though the world has exhaled and shifted,
and i am left standing in its echo,
unsure if i am guest, ghost, or dream.

everything changes but nothing turns out new—
a paradox stitched into the skin of time,
where the river runs and runs, yet always
returns to drink from its own mouth.

the seasons fracture, the stars rearrange,
but the marrow of the world stays the same,
an old song repeating beneath the noise,
etched deeper each time it is sung.

and what of growth, of progress, of ascent,
if every step forward spirals back again?
perhaps the shifting is only within us,
or perhaps even that is a dream we name "becoming."

so the wheel turns, and we mistake its motion
for a path—yet when the dust clears,
it may be we have gone nowhere at all,
only circling the echo of a question
that was never meant to be answered.

in the disorderly sea of voices,
a ripple of quiet—
a moment of disturbance,
a pause in the riot.

amidst the clamour,
a peculiar hush unfurls,
a whispering disturbance
in the shouting world.

the echoes of silence
speak louder than the noise—
a subtle rebellion
that disrupts the vocal poise.

in this quiet interlude,
where tumult swirls,
a momentary disturbance
in the shouting world.

whispers in the stillness,
a clandestine affair—
a quiet disruption
in the midst of blaring blare.

in the loud symphony,
where chaos swirls,
a moment of hushed disturbance
in the shouting world.

in the stillness of the night's eerie hush,
a truth emerges—sudden, uninvited.
reality bends,
twists in unfamiliar ways,
as shadows move
in the fractured light.

the world tilts—
a surreal scene
where the boundaries of sanity
shudder and slide.

in the flicker of an eye,
everything is revealed:
a cosmic secret
long held in silence.

minds bewildered,
hearts unsteady,
we stand before the truth—
strange, unending,
its glow both cold
and alive.

i am the writer, but you'll be my words,
a curious dance in the theatre of creation,
where roles blur and identities merge,
and the boundaries between us dissolve.

in the tapestry of our shared existence,
you become the ink that stains my pages,
the whispered secrets that fill the silence,
and the melodies that linger in the air.

but what happens when the story takes an unexpected turn,
and the characters rebel against their creator,
leaving me to chase shadows in the night,
and grapple with the ghosts of what could have been?

i am the architect of our narrative,
but you are the muse that inspires,
guiding my hand as i navigate the labyrinth,
and weaving yourself into the fabric of my dreams.

so let us embrace this strange alchemy,
where i am the vessel and you are the essence,
for in the merging of our souls,
we find the magic that breathes life into our story.

in the kaleidoscopic carnival of altered reality,
technicolour unicorns tap-danced on clouds
of psychedelic cotton candy,
serenading a swirling galaxy
of interdimensional fireflies
with melodies composed
of liquid stardust.

cold mornings,
twisted lullabies
and floral scents.
they linger in the air,
sweet enough to hide
what's rotting beneath.

for those who dream of stranger worlds,
they know that reality's bounds
are only a show.

in the depths of their minds,
they roam unfurled—
forever lost
in the strange, surreal world.

but the strange will not release them,
it keeps them wandering halls
that have no doors—
only mirrors,
and reflections they no longer recognize.

"i'm proud of myself in a bad way,"
a confession sharpened into a whisper,
an echo that folds in on itself,
sour and sweet at once.

pride—what is it but a blade
that cuts both hand and heart,
leaving me half triumphant,
half undone?

to be proud of the ruin i've built,
the scars i carry like trophies,
the choices i knew were wrong
yet claimed as mine—
is this not pride, too?

perhaps it is only the human way
to glory in our fractures,
to polish the cracks until they gleam,
and call the wound a kind of crown.

but what if pride is never clean,
never holy, never whole—
just another shadow we cradle,
mistaking its weight for worth?

"i'll be fine once i get it," she whispers
into the hollow of the night,
a mantra stitched from longing,
threadbare and trembling in her chest.

but what is "it"? a shape without form,
a promise blurred on the horizon,
a shadow she chases until her breath
breaks into splinters of silence.

perhaps "it" is nothing at all—
just a phantom carved by hunger,
a mirage in the desert of desire,
always ahead, never in hand.

and yet, she runs,
knowing each step pulls her further
from the ground beneath her feet,
from the quiet pulse of the present.

in the end, will she ever touch it?
or will "it" dissolve at her fingertips,
revealing only the emptiness
she carried all along?

i wrote so much shit, i wouldn't dare to recite—
words that throb like wounds beneath the skin,
scribbles etched in fever, half delirium,
half a mirror i refuse to face.

each line, a ghost of something i betrayed,
each fragment, a confession carved in code.
to speak them would be to shatter the silence,
to summon shadows i've barely kept asleep.

so i let the ink rot in its quiet grave,
pages curling into the weight of their own truth,
letters dissolving into ash and static—
proof that some things are meant
to die inside you, unheard.

i'm everywhere but here—
nothing more than an idea,
a spectre lingering on the fringes of reality,
a whisper in the wind,
a shadow that refuses to cast.

in the realm of abstraction, i persist,
a concept without bone or breath,
a figment born of thought alone,
a pulse in the veins of the intangible.

and yet, despite my weightless nature,
i thread myself through the fabric of existence,
woven between the moments,
binding together what should never meet.

perhaps i am only a reflection
of the mind's uncharted expanse,
proof that imagination
is the closest we ever come to truth.

i am not a body but a sign,
a flicker, a symbol,
a shifting horizon at the edge of perception.

for what is real,
if not the shape we give it?
and what we call perception
is only the mirror turning back,
offering us our own shadow in return.

i step toward tomorrow to escape yesterday,
yet the ground beneath me folds into now—
a cruel loop where every door is a mirror,
and each reflection drags the past behind.

the future gleams like a distant shore,
but the tide pulls me back to the same sand,
the same footprints dissolving, reforming,
as if time itself mocks my retreat.

what is escape, if the present is a cage
built from shadows of what i've fled?
what is freedom, if every horizon bends
into the narrow corridor of here?

still, i walk—because to stop is worse,
because even in the endless present
there is the faint illusion of motion,
a whisper that the cycle might break.

v. grey

sometimes minds overflow—
a self-portrait in letters,
drawn in the margins
of sleepless nights.

no one whispered of days
draped in shades of grey,
where the heart wrestles
with storms it cannot abide.

no one warned
of the weight of silent tears,
or the loneliness
that seeps through.

no one foretold of the darkness
that descends
when the world seems
to reach its silent ends.

yet in these days
of unforeseen despair,
i find resilience—
and amidst the chaos,
i learn to dream.

let me step past the edge of the surface,
i want to sink further into you—
and from the depth, through the deep,
my words of whispers
will reach you.

you will feel them
curl around your bones,
slipping between the quiet spaces
where even your shadow
does not follow.

when they first told us what to be,
they taught us to dream—
visions grand, hopes bright enough to blind.

but in the maze of existence,
we are given no map
to navigate the depths of the mind.

dreams painted in gold and blue
fade into the sharper shades of reality.
they told us to reach for the stars,
but not how to move through
the depths of love.

in dreams, we soar,
but in waking hours,
we stumble.

they gave us wings
but not the ground
to stand on when the tempests rise.

in chasing dreams,
we lost sight
of the essence of being—

for they taught us to dream,
but never to see
that being ourselves
was the truest key.

why am i doing it again,
if only i could start where i ended,
but i'm ending up starting again.

the cycle does not break,
it just learns new ways
to disguise itself.

reside within. in this darkness,
a haunting opus of whispers
and unseen movements increases.

it is a realm where uncertainties take shape
and visions come alive—
where the unknown moves with its gloomy charm,
and the line between reality and the dream
blurs into an encouraging depth.

i've been present in a different world.
i tried to come home, but i never really arrived—
i got lost along the way.

maybe my memories are all the home
i get in this world.

don't listen to me for too long,
you'll fall in love—
not with me, but with the
world within me.

i'm not from around here,
but you won't notice
until i vanish.

and when i'm gone,
you will search for me
in every silence,
finding pieces
that were never mine to give.

in the labyrinth of existence, i roam,
a stranger in a world that doesn't feel like home.
this realm, with its rules and decree,
seems alien—never meant for me.

the colours are too bright, the silence too loud.
in the constant noise, i remain apart.
each step i take,
i question my place
in this vast and shifting dance.

the echoes of my voice fade,
lost in the noise this world creates.
in the strangeness of it all,
i find a quiet solace
in being something else.

in the quiet search
to understand what's coming,
i walked across a dim landscape.

each step echoed,
haunted by the strange beauty
of trying to find the end
before it happens.

in the depths of our minds, hidden away,
live the thoughts we don't show.

in the quiet,
these are the ones we return to—
the ones we keep close,
the ones that will not let us go.

crashed down, right here with her,
and the scent of something other than
what i'm used to... the savour of desire
still scorching on my lower lip.

collapsed—
like she fell from beyond.
her mystery
is tying my thoughts around her;
even the phantoms must wonder
where she keeps her wings.

though i start to feel the space and distance,
she whispers, *we remain alone, come look inside me.*

i   l o s t   it   a l l   t h e r e.

in the caverns of my mind,
your presence stays—
a puzzle unsolved,
its edges always shifting.

i strain to read
the currents of your thoughts,
but your inner world
remains untouched by light.

in the shadows of doubt,
i search for a clue,
yet every glance,
every word,
is only a fragment—
a reflection
of something i cannot hold.

like glass fractured,
you scatter in all directions,
and i struggle
to gather the pieces.

what you think of me
slips further from reach,
lost in the labyrinth
where your thoughts turn.

in the enigma of your mind,
i am adrift—
not knowing if i am welcome,
or only passing through.

we ignore truth for temporary happiness—
a fleeting comfort
in the face of harsh reality.

we choose illusion over confrontation,
burying our heads
in the sand of denial.

beneath the surface of contentment
lies a simmering unease,
a quiet doubt,
as we trade the clarity of truth
for the opiate of momentary pleasure—
brief, insubstantial.

and so we wander the labyrinth of our lives,
blinded by the pull of temporary satisfaction,
lost in the fog of our own deception,
uncertain where the path of lies will take us.

truth is a harsh mistress—
demanding, unforgiving—
but in her embrace
is the promise of liberation:
the chance to break free
from the shackles of illusion,
to face the world
with open eyes.

still,
we turn away,
seeking refuge in shadows,
preferring the comfort of ignorance
to the harsh light
of reality's gaze.

"i'm not even sure why i'm here anymore,"
he murmurs, a whisper swallowed by the void,
a question cast into the abyss
with no echo to return it.

purpose shifts like sand in a restless wind,
a shape half-seen, dissolving at the edges,
mocking the mind that dares to grasp it.

each step forward feels like retracing,
each moment borrowed from a clock
that refuses to reveal its face.

perhaps the reason was never there,
or perhaps it waits, obscured,
behind curtains too heavy to draw.

yet he walks on, not from certainty
but from the inertia of being alive,
as if movement itself were a kind of answer.

and in this lies the cruelest paradox:
that meaning may not exist,
and yet the search will not release him—
a wandering boundless,
a seeking that defines the seeker,
long after the question has turned to ash.

fly high, they said, with voices like whispers in the wind,
echoing through the hollow chambers of my mind,
a summons to touch the heavens,
to press my fingertips against the cold fire of stars.

but what does it mean, to rise above,
in a world shackled by gravity and sorrow,
where dreams fracture like glass in the dark,
and hope flickers, a fragile flame trembling in silence?

i spread my wings and leap into the abyss,
the wind rushing sharp against my face,
the exhilaration of freedom singing in my veins,
as i ascend into the boundless expanse of night.

yet even as i climb, i feel the weight—
a world pressing like stone upon my shoulders,
while shadows of doubt gnaw at the edges of thought,
reminding me that wings are as fragile as faith.

still, i push into the strangeness of the sky,
driven by a hunger that defies reason,
a yearning to dissolve the borders of myself,
and embrace the vast, indifferent universe.

for even in this haunting ascent,
there is beauty, sharp and untamed,
and in the abyss of the soul,
a strength born of surrender.

so let me fly, not to conquer the heavens,
but to lose myself in them—
for in the strangeness of the unknown
there is freedom,
and there is truth.

where in our minds do we put what we can't understand,
a question that echoes in the corridors of thought,
lost in the labyrinth of our own confusion,
as we grapple with the enigma of existence.

do we bury it deep, in the recesses of our subconscious,
hoping it will fade into the background noise,
or do we let it linger, a constant reminder
of the limits of our understanding?

in the tangled web of our thoughts,
there are no easy answers, only more questions,
as we wrestle with the complexities of the human condition,
and the mysteries that lie beyond our grasp.

but still, we search for meaning,
in the chaos of our confusion, hoping to find some
semblance of clarity, in the tangled mess of our thoughts.

for in the midst of our uncertainty,
there is a strange comfort in the chaos,
a reminder that we are all stumbling
through the darkness of our own minds.

eye contact the kiss of shy people—
a fleeting connection in a world of silence,
where words falter
and hearts speak in whispers,
lost in the expanse of unspoken desire.

in the quiet depths of hesitant gazes
lies a universe of longing and uncertainty.
each glance a brushstroke
on the canvas of possibility,
too fragile to bear
the weight of expectation.

for the shy,
it is a delicate dance—
navigating the minefield
of unspoken emotion,
where a single look
can ignite or extinguish
the flickering flame of hope.

and so we linger
in the shadows we create,
afraid to reach out,
yet longing to be seen.

for in the silence
of timid glances
lies the echo of a love
that dares not speak its name.

time moves on,
relentless in its passage.
seasons shift,
casting shadows across our stay.

slowly,
almost without notice,
our paths pulled apart—
the bond we held
fractured and submerged.

in quiet moments,
i see it clearly:
forever is only an idea
we tell ourselves.

yet in the echoes
of what we shared,
i still find a strange solace.
our time together has passed,
but the moments remain—
frozen in the shape they once held.

there was a time
i believed i would know you always,
and in that brief span,
we were bound.

alone—
a sanctuary of tranquil reprieve,
a solace only solitude can conceive.

in the quiet,
where thoughts gently weave,
alone feels good—
an embrace i won't leave.

a company of one,
a sweet solitude,
in the calm retreat
where silence is pursued.

to break the peace,
someone must exude
something sweeter than solitude,
where quiet is renewed.

for in the company of self,
a gentle grace—
alone feels good,
a sacred, quiet space.

if someone steps in,
their sweetness must trace
a melody softer
than my solitary embrace.

it's the possibility of having a dream come true
that makes life interesting—
a glimmer of hope
in the darkness of uncertainty,
a beacon guiding us
through the labyrinth of existence.

but what happens when the dream fades?
when the light dims
and the path grows faint,
leaving us stranded
in the void of disillusion—
where shattered hopes
litter the ground like broken glass?

we cling to the fragments,
desperate to salvage
some semblance of meaning,
but the pieces slip through our fingers
like sand—
leaving us empty-handed
and alone.

and yet,
in the quiet moments of despair,
there is solace in the dream itself—
in the possibility
of what could have been,
even as reality
slips into the shadows.

seeking a black hole to a kinder dimension,
a quest for escape from the confines of reality,
where the laws of physics bend and warp,
and the boundaries of existence blur and dissolve.

in the depths of space-time, where the fabric of reality frays,
we search for a doorway to another realm,
where pain and suffering are but distant memories,
and the weight of the world is lifted from our shoulders.

but as we peer into the abyss, we are confronted
with the stark reality of our own mortality,
and the futility of our quest for escape,
for there is no refuge from the human condition.

yet still we seek, driven by the hope
that somewhere beyond the event horizon
lies a sanctuary, a haven of peace and tranquility,
where we can find solace in the embrace of the unknown.

but perhaps the true journey lies not in escape,
but in the acceptance of our own limitations,
and the recognition that it is within ourselves
that we must find the courage to face our fears.

alone i stand
at the precipice of time—
a seeker of endings,
a quest sublime.

for to begin anew,
i must first find
the closure
to what's left behind.

through winding paths
and shadows deep,
i tread alone
where secrets sleep.

in the depths of darkness,
i roam
to find the key
that leads me home.

for endings hold
the seeds of new starts—
a cycle unbroken
from which life imparts.

so i alone
must seek the end,
to embrace beginnings
around the bend.

time—
a construct woven
into the fabric of existence,
an illusion of the mind,
a perplexing persistence.

in the vast expanse of consciousness,
a holographic dance—
a simulation set in linear time,
where emotions intensify.

moments unfold
in the tapestry of perception,
each experience a lesson,
a quiet introspection.

time, a vessel
for the exploration of the soul—
a journey through emotions,
making us whole.

linear time guides us
through the depths of being,
as we navigate
the spectrum of feeling.

in this hologram of existence,
we ponder and reflect
on the nature of time—
a concept we intersect.

as i fall back deeper into a state,
trying to find the things i'm feeling.

a sigh of relief, now nothing but a memory—
a thin, crooked smile, as she now dances
to her own melody.

i watch from the quiet,
each step she takes
pulling her further
into a place
i will never follow.

within the vast expanse of my mind's sea,
thoughts move in currents—
restless, untamed.

beneath the surface,
where the water darkens,
lies a world unseen.

like the ocean's depths,
my thoughts drift and twist,
a labyrinth without walls.

each wave that breaks
sends new fragments ashore,
then pulls them back again.

beyond the surface,
where the light dissolves,
is a realm of shadow,
where mysteries gather and wait.

in the depths of my mind,
a silent ocean swells—
its secrets kept
until time decides to speak.

in the stillness of the night,
echoes move low through the air—
a familiar sensation,
a feeling i've come to know.

again, i drift through the surreal,
a stranger to my own skin,
wandering without direction.

the world turns in fractured colour,
but inside,
a quiet unrest spreads,
slow and unshaped.

i move as a passenger
through this enigmatic ride,
lost in the corridors of thought
where truths disappear.

feeling strange again,
as if i've lost my way—
as if direction itself
has turned its back on me,
and i'm caught
between the solid and the dream.

yet somewhere in the unfamiliar
a quiet recognition lingers—
the sense
that even here,
something waits to be found.

in the twilight of eternity,
where time dissolves,
an ending without an end
unfolds quietly.

no boundaries contain
its silent descent—
it wraps the cosmos
in a veiled intent.

a paradox of shadow and light,
where day and night converge
without destination.

each moment becomes a fragment,
a shard of something whole,
yet the puzzle remains incomplete.

threads of infinity
intertwine without knowing,
and we wander
through an infinite blend—
seeking solace
in the ending without an end.

in its depths,
a strange grace lingers.
we lean into the void,
and let it hold us.

that's why some stories have to end in the middle—
paused mid-breath,
the air heavy with what might have come next.

there are chapters
that guard their own endings,
sentences that refuse to be spoken,
turning to silence.

sometimes the plot twists
not to break us,
but to lead us somewhere
we were never meant to see.

the narrative veers off the map,
into a landscape without borders,
where time folds in on itself
and the horizon is just a suggestion.

we are left standing
in the stillness after the turning page,
aware of the silence,
but certain it holds more
than we are ready to know.

i'm drawn to the peace of feeling nothing,
but feeling nothing can quickly become
really real...

"real"...
there's that word again.

to the world, it's not supposed to be like this.
i know it doesn't make sense,
the way the world can let you fall.

and when you hit the ground,
no one asks
if you were pushed,
or if you jumped.

in the odd realm where shadows hold court,
a soul romanticizes the darkness—
a peculiar sport.

moonbeams and whispers,
their clandestine mates,
in the strange romance
where darkness contemplates.

the night becomes a canvas
for their unusual delight,
stars as verses in a love poem
written in the dark.

they find solace in the silence
that the shadows weave,
romanticizing the darkness—
an eccentric reprieve.

in the peculiar embrace of ebony hue,
they discover beauty
where others see taboo.

a dance with the shadows,
a flirtation with the night—
romancing the darkness,
a peculiar delight.

in the quiet spaces
where sadness once resided,
a soft ending unfolds,
where tears have subsided.

no lingering echoes
of sorrow or despair,
just a tender departure—
a breath of mended air.

gentle rays of hope
pierce through the gloom,
as the weight of sadness
finds a tranquil room.

no tumultuous waves
of grief or strife,
only a serene dissolve—
the softening of life.

the sighs of sorrow
whisper a muted goodbye,
fading like a distant,
melancholic sigh.

in the soft ending,
where healing threads embark,
a gentle closure to the sadness,
a tender embark.

a higher view—
the discomfort we cannot yet avoid,
needing to make the most
of the things we can't ignore.

and still,
we pretend it's a choice,
as if turning away
could unmake what waits for us.

but the horizon does not blink,
and the air tastes the same,
no matter how far we try to run.

we are but transient shadows
in the passage of time—
a fleeting moment,
a breath in life's paradigm.

in the cosmic dance,
we shimmer and fade,
moments dissolving
in the ever-shifting drift.

it makes sense at night;
please forgive me
if i don't talk much at times.
it's loud enough in my head.

at the end of time,
in the fading light's embrace,
we reminisce of better days—
a bittersweet trace.

in the quiet surrender
to the twilight's sway,
memories of brighter moments
gently fade away.

the past is obscure, and reality unidentified.
in a world where secrets are overgrown,
a story untold, forever sad—
deep in the depths of the night,
we never had.

on a long path,
in a short existence,
we are our own presence—
in a world where all faces
seem to have the same
familiar glimmer.

in the enigma's embrace,
a soft ending unfurls—
a mysterious chapter
whispers its final swirl.

no increase of secrets,
no impressive finale,
just a quiet unravelling—
a mystique's slow ballet.

shadows recede
in a gentle retreat,
as mysteries dissolve
in a tender defeat.

the unknown, once veiled
in a cryptic dance,
softly fades away,
leaving a lingering trance.

no dramatic revelation,
only a subtle dissolve—
in the soft ending,
where mysteries evolve.

the arcane whispers
a final hushed refrain,
as the mysterious fades—
a soft ending's gain.

in the quiet corners
where shadows quietly converse,
a soul finds solace—
an unconventional universe.

lover of the darkness,
where the night is a friend,
embracing the shadows—
a romance without end.

moonlit paths become
the silent lanes they tread,
stars as confidants
in the vast night spread.

a strange affair with shadows,
an intimate tryst,
in the love for darkness—
an unusual twist.

the quiet becomes a sanctuary,
a secret bower;
they find beauty in the night,
in its mysterious power.

a whispering symphony
where shadows gently sway—
in the love for darkness,
they find peace in the grey.

as we are in the twilight of reality,
just unearthed fragments of our existence—
we embark on a peculiar journey
through the passages of the surreal.

experiencing in hues unseen by worldly eyes,
echoed with the laughter of make-believe friends
and temporary acquaintances,
this glimmer becomes a portal to realms
where logic tangled with the illogical
is only a memory of what once was.

it all brings a mixture of characters and love too,
which wears a surreal disguise.
relationships are like abstract paintings—
beautiful in chaos, inexplicable in form.

heartbreaks feel like cosmic collisions,
each tear and hurt like a supernova
in the vast expanse of emotions.

this is a lullaby for the restless,
in the urban pulse where we find our solace
beneath the streetlights' muted glow.

a city whispers secrets we tend not to know,
silent footsteps on the midnight streets...

now, in the autumn of our existence,
amidst the chaos, a moment frozen in time—
what a pity these city lights glow.

the darkness changes us—
in the end, we will not recognize
the shape we are.

it molds us like wet earth,
pressing its weight into our bones,
etching its designs in places
no light can reach.

in the crucible of shadow,
we are transformed.
the silence grows teeth,
the stillness hums with intent,
and the power it holds
binds itself to us,
threading through every thought,
every breath.

but as we step out
from whatever place we have been,
we find the edges of ourselves
blurred and strange.

the familiar outline
of who we once were
is gone—
replaced by something
that does not speak its name.

and yet, in this unfamiliarity,
there is a pull,
a beauty,
a whisper that perhaps
this is what we were meant to be.

or perhaps,
this is what it wanted us to become.

it's a long path, but a short life—
a melancholy refrain.
another cold morning in tokyo,
where shadows linger.

to seek out the end,
a prelude to a forlorn beginning,
my heart entangled
in a bittersweet dance with time.

amidst the city's chill,
my mind is captive to musings,
in awe of the unalterable,
etched in the soul.

i could spill words,
unravel my heart's secret cadence,
yet fear that understanding
will always elude,
like a phantom.

living my life surrounded
by the flicker of hopeful light,
goodbyes—poignant
as a melancholy riddle—
echo through the corridors of parting.

stuck in my mind,
a haunting refrain
of farewells unsaid.

in the quiet exhale of the world's last breath,
a soft ending unfurls—
a gentle embrace of death.

no cataclysmic roars or tumultuous cries,
just a tender dissolve
as the final curtain lies.

sunset hues linger
in a poignant caress,
as constellations shimmer
in the cosmic recess.

the world sighs—
a lullaby of fading dreams,
slipping quietly
into celestial streams.

mountains bow,
oceans cradle the hushed goodbye,
in the soft ending,
where echoes gently lie.

nature's poem
whispered in rustling leaves,
a tranquil departure
as the world softly heaves.

no thunderous finale,
only serenity profound—
the last chapter of earth
in silence bound.

soft ripples in the cosmic pond,
a gentle swirl,
a tender conclusion
to the soft ending of the world.

that's why some stories have to end in the middle—
a bitter truth whispered in the silence of loss,
where hope fades like a dying ember,
and dreams dissolve into the void of oblivion.

in the pages of our lives,
there are chapters that remain forever unfinished,
sentences left hanging in the air—
waiting for resolution,
but doomed to remain incomplete.

sometimes, the plot twists unexpectedly,
the narrative veers off course,
and we find ourselves stranded
in the wilderness of uncertainty,
with no map to guide us back
to familiar shores.

we mourn the endings that never came,
the resolutions that slipped through our hands,
as we come to accept
that some stories are meant
to remain unfinished.

yet even in the weight of this sorrow,
a glimmer remains—
for in the silence of the unwritten ending
lies the possibility
of a new beginning.

the end will be ironic, a twist of fate
in the grand narrative of existence,
where the lines between comedy and tragedy
blur and intertwine like threads in a tapestry.

for what is life but a series of paradoxes,
a dance of light and shadow, joy and sorrow,
where the unexpected lurks around every corner,
and irony is the currency of the cosmos?

in the final act of the cosmic drama,
we may find ourselves confronted with the absurd,
as the threads of destiny weave together
in a tapestry of cosmic coincidence.

yet amidst the chaos and confusion,
there lies a strange comfort in the irony,
for it reminds us that life is not meant to be understood,
but embraced with all its contradictions and complexities.

so let us embrace the irony of our existence,
and find meaning in the midst of the absurd,
for in the end, it is not the destination that matters,
but the journey itself, and the lessons we learn along the way.

i take comfort in knowing that none of it matters—
or perhaps it does, in ways too vast for us to name.

we are both the dust and the hand that scatters it,
a fleeting pattern in an endless and indifferent sky.

the universe leans over us without voice or face,
its silence not cruel, but unreadable,
as if it holds an answer that changes
the moment we come close to hearing it.

what does it matter if we rise or fall,
when the stars themselves are uncertain
of why they burn, or if they burn at all?
even light seems unsure of where it belongs.

and yet, there is a strange solace in this—
in knowing the script may never be written,
that we drift through something infinite
without ever touching its edges.

so we walk,
neither lost nor found,
carrying the quiet suspicion
that meaning is both everywhere
and nowhere at once.

it isn't such a bad place for things to end,
beneath the silence where echoes fold inwards,
where the last word dissolves before it's heard
and the air tastes faintly of unfinished thought.

endings are not explosions but fade-outs,
threads unspooled into the quiet fabric,
a curtain falling without applause,
the lights dimming though no one leaves their seat.

perhaps it is mercy to conclude here,
in the soft confusion of half-shadows,
where nothing is final but nothing remains,
where memory hums like a wire in the dark.

it isn't such a bad place for things to end—
in the grey distance, in the trembling pause,
where the unfinished becomes its own completion
and departure feels strangely like return.

when the last words are spoken,
the echo of silence fills the space.

was it an ending,
or the beginning
of something unnamed, unfinished?

perhaps the silence is the message—
a truth too vast for language,
or nothing at all.

i wonder if endings
were ever real,
or if all we hold
is the pause
between vanishing thoughts.

m.d.p

h.f

b.s.n.c

k.c

s.e

c.f.k

a.k.s

w.k

m.m

c.c.c

x.k

in the silence
between thought and breath
there lies a heavy truth

in black
waits the end

STARLING

www.ingramcontent.com/pod-product-compliance
Lightning Source LLC
Chambersburg PA
CBHW071500070426
42452CB00041B/1977